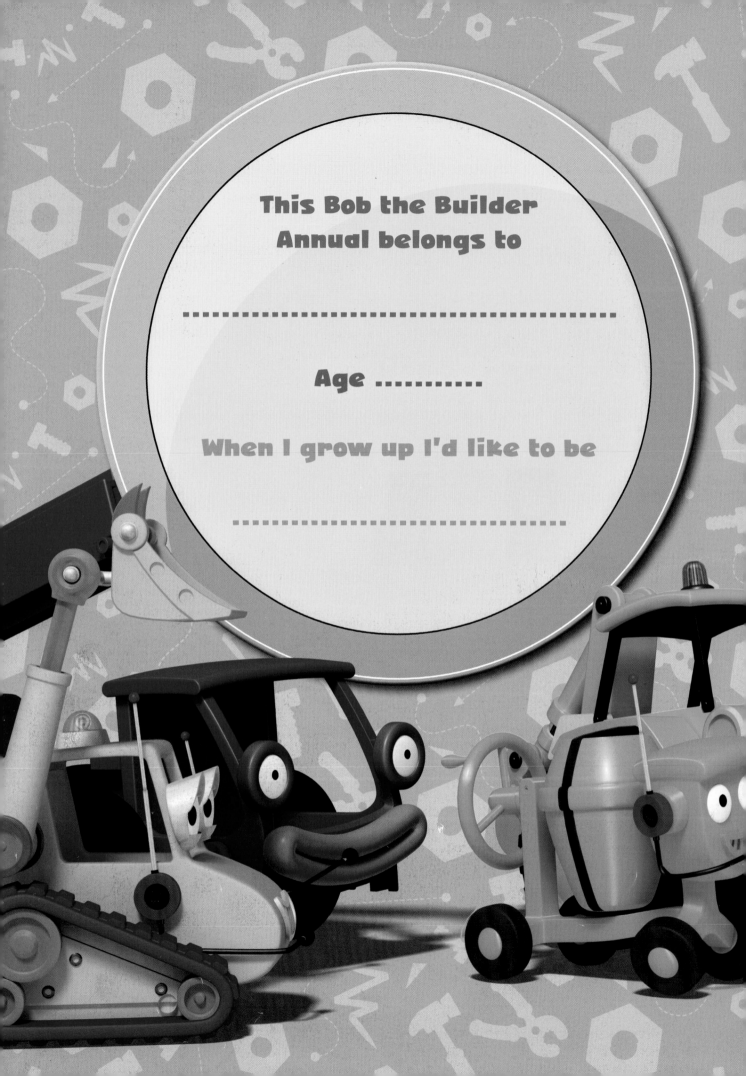

This Bob the Builder
Annual belongs to

....

Age ....

When I grow up I'd like to be

....

Bob the Builder™

ANNUAL 2013

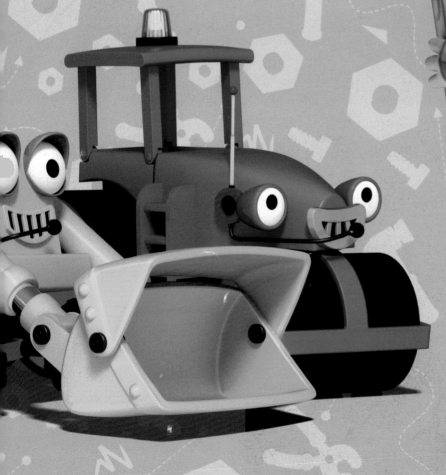

OK TEAM! LET'S GET TO WORK!

First published in Great Britain 2012
by Egmont UK Limited
239 Kensington High Street, London W8 6SA

Written by Lizzie Catford • Designed by Pritty Ramjee • Photography by Beth Harwood

Based on the television series Bob the Builder
© 2012 HIT Entertainment Limited and Keith Chapman.
All rights reserved. The Bob the Builder name and character, related characters
and riveted logo are trademarks of HIT Entertainment Limited.

ISBN 978 1 4052 6336 8
51509/2
Printed in Italy

Adult supervision is recommended when glue, paint, scissors and other sharp points are in use.

CONTENTS

Star in
your very
own

**Bob the
Builder
book!**

★ www.egmont.co.uk/pod ★

MEET the Team!

Scoop

Muck

Roley

There isn't a lump or a bump that Roley the steamroller can't flatten.

The bigger the job the better, for big digger Scoop.

Muck, the big red dump truck, loves all the really muddy jobs.

Bob the Builder

Scratch

Dizzy

With his hard hat and tool belt on, Bob is ready to fix anything.

Little Scratch can't wait to be a big digger like Scoop and Muck.

Whizzy Dizzy is always busy, mixing up the best cement in town.

9

AROUND Fixham

Bob and the machines live in the seaside town of Fixham Harbour. Fixham is a happy town. Bob has lots of friends and neighbours there.

Farmer Pickles

Farmer Pickles lives on the farm with his tractor Travis, Scruffty the dog and Spud.

Mrs Toosey

Mrs Toosey runs Fixham's Toy Shop. She sells lots of unusual and exciting toys.

David Mockney

David Mockney is a local artist. He is in charge of Fixham Museum.

Ela

Ela is a teacher. She works with the children at Fixham school.

Brad Rad

Brad Rad is a lifeguard. He helps anyone who gets into trouble at the beach.

Mr Bentley

Mr Bentley always has a new passion! His latest craze is football. He manages the local team, Fixham Rovers.

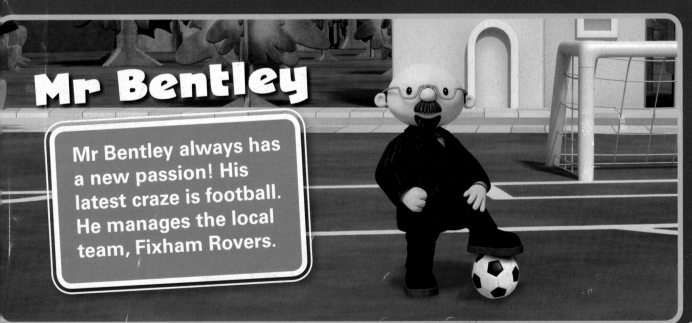

SCOOP the Artist

"I've just had a call from David Mockney, the artist," said Bob to the team one morning. "He needs a whole new room built on the side of Fixham Museum – **today**!"

"Ohh! An artist!" stammered Scoop. "They paint pictures, don't they?"

"Yes," said Bob. "But David Mockey doesn't just paint, he's a sculptor, too. He makes models of things."

Morning, team!

The team rushed over to the museum.

At the museum, Scoop spotted one of the sculptures. **"David Mockney is good at so many things. All I can do is dig,"** he said, sadly.

But there was no time to look at the art. There was work to be done!

Bob showed the team where to get started.

Just then, David Mockney came out of the museum. **"I've decided to paint a picture on the side wall of the new building,"** he announced.

Scoop rushed up to meet the artist. **"How about using a sunny yellow paint**?" he said, quickly.

"Fabulous idea," replied David Mockney.

David Mockney asked Bob if he could borrow Scoop to help him go to the Supplier's Yard to buy the paint for his new picture.

"OK," said Bob. **"But don't be too long, Scoop – there's lots of work to do."**

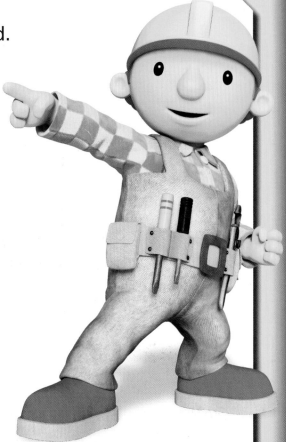

Scoop was so excited! He wanted to be a famous artist just like David Mockey.

"Can we paint a picture now?" Scoop asked, as they drove to the Supplier's Yard. **"Then you could teach me how to be a great artist like you!"**

"We really should hurry," said the artist. **"But, oh well, why not?"**

David Mockney set up his easel, canvas and paints. He painted one picture, and then another and then another. Scoop kept suggesting new things for him to paint. He was so happy to be watching a **real artist** at work.

That's amazing!

Back at the museum the team were working hard. Roley rolled the ground flat. Scratch and Muck dug out the foundations and Dizzy filled them in.

"I wonder where Scoop has got to?" said Bob. **"This is a tough job and we need his help."**

Meanwhile, Scoop had asked David Mockney to paint so many pictures that when they got to the Supplier's Yard it had closed for the day.

"Oh, no," cried Scoop. **"I wanted to learn to be an artist, so I forgot about the job. It's all my fault."**

Scoop drove sadly back to the museum.

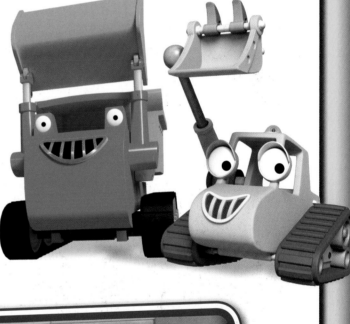

When Scoop and Mr Mockney got back to the museum the new building was nearly finished.

"Thank goodness you're back, Scoop," said Bob when he saw him. **"Can you dig the flower-beds as quickly as you can?"**

"I'll dig faster than I've ever dug before," promised Scoop.

"I'm really sorry, Mr Mockney," he added. **"I got carried away wanting to be an artist and now we haven't got the paint for your big picture. I suppose I'm just a digger, not an artist …"**

"Don't worry," replied the artist. **"I'll help to plant the flowers."**

Scoop set to work digging out the flower-beds while the others planted the flowers. When they all stood back to admire their work they couldn't believe their eyes. Scoop had dug the flower-bed in the shape of a flower. It looked **amazing!**

"I don't need to paint my picture now," said the artist. "We've made a fantastic flower-bed picture instead. Scoop – you're a **natural artist**!"

"It's great being an artist," Scoop said to his friends, "but digging the flower-bed has reminded me – being a digger is the best job in the world!"

SUNNY Scoop Collage

David Mockney is making a collage of Scoop. Why don't you make one too?

1

Draw an outline of Scoop. You can trace or use the picture of Scoop on the opposite page. Cut it out and stick it onto a large sheet of paper.

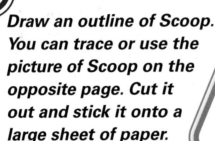

You will need:

- Coloured tissue paper, including yellow, black and white
- a large sheet of plain paper
- scissors
- glue

2

Tear up the tissue paper into small pieces. Scrunch up the pieces into small balls. Stick the balls of tissue paper onto your outline of Scoop.

3

Make sure you follow the lines and put your colours in the right places.

A sunny Scoop collage makes a great present!

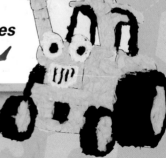

COLOUR Mix-up!

Look carefully at this picture of Bob and Wendy doing some painting. Can you spot **5** colours that have gone wrong in the picture?

Answers on page 68.

GET Ready with Bob

Help Bob get the job done by joining in and miming all the actions.

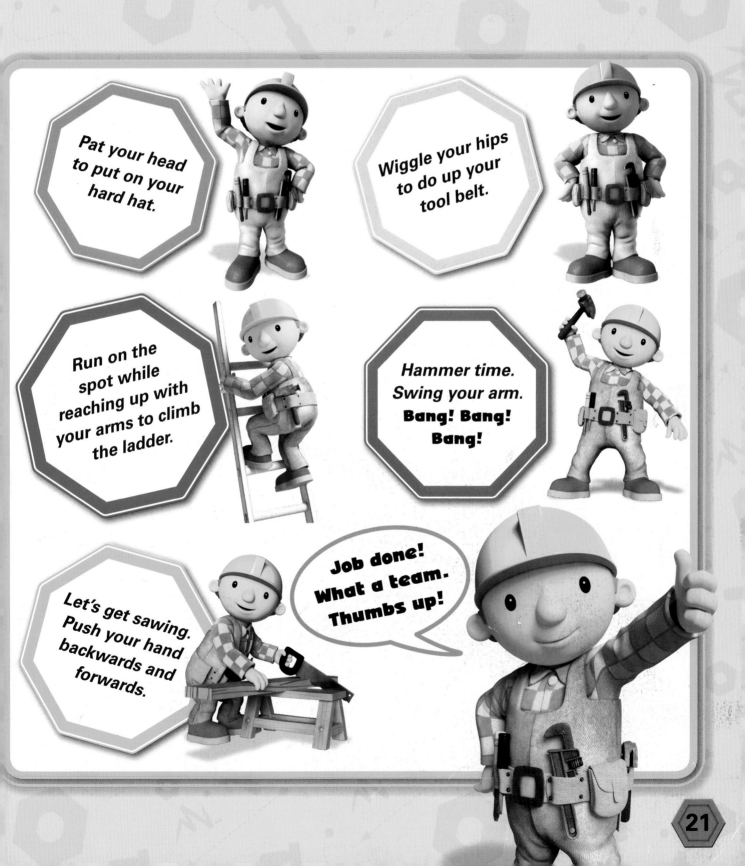

Pat your head to put on your hard hat.

Wiggle your hips to do up your tool belt.

Run on the spot while reaching up with your arms to climb the ladder.

Hammer time. Swing your arm. **Bang! Bang! Bang!**

Let's get sawing. Push your hand backwards and forwards.

Job done! What a team. Thumbs up!

MUCK'S Beach Tower

Bright and early, Bob called Scoop and Lofty. Their help was needed **at the beach**! They were going to build Brad Rad a new lifeguard tower.

"Awww!" chorused the other machines. They wanted to go to the beach too.

"We could have built sandcastles!" sniffed Muck.

"But you can all come!" said Wendy.

At the beach Bob told Scoop and Lofty what they needed to do. First, they would build the tower. Then they would dig foundations. Last of all, they would lift the tower into place. They got down to work, while the other machines went to play.

Nearby, Muck discovered a pile of driftwood. He decided to make a driftwood **castle**!

"Even better than a sandcastle!" Muck chuckled to himself. He zipped off to find a good spot to build it.

He hadn't gone far when he bumped into Dizzy, Roley and Scratch. They were building a sandcastle together and wanted Muck to join in.

"Um, do you mind if I build my own castle?" asked Muck.

They didn't mind, but wondered if he had a special plan.

"Yeah!" boasted Muck. **"It's going to be the best castle ever!"**

Meanwhile, Bob, Lofty and Scoop were ready to start on the foundations.

"We'll make them strong using large boulders," said Bob. **"But we'll need Muck's help. I'll ask him to collect the boulders from the Supplier's Yard."**

Muck didn't mind going to the Supplier's Yard. When he got there he asked for 3 extra boulders. He wanted to give his castle a strong foundation, just like Brad's tower!

Back at the beach, Muck put his 3 boulders to one side.

Then he dug a big hole for the tower foundations and filled it up with the rest of the boulders.

Soon it was time to raise the tower! Lofty pushed and Muck pulled, until the tower was upright.

"Hmm …" said Bob. **"Nearly there. It just needs a sunshade."**

And he set about making one.

Just then, there was a loud cheer. It was the other machines. They'd finished their sandcastle and it looked **fantastic**!

"Oh, no," thought Muck. **"I must build my castle."**

He quickly dug a hole for his foundations. But he couldn't see his 3 boulders anywhere.

Muck looked everywhere. But the other machines had built their sandcastle in front of his boulders and they were **hidden**!

"I must have put them in the tower foundations by mistake," Muck decided, and he took out 3 boulders.

Then he quickly built his driftwood castle. It looked amazing!

Meanwhile, Bob had finished the sunshade. The tower was finally ready! Brad climbed up onto the platform. But when he sat down, there was a loud **creaking** noise. And the tower started to wobble.

"Muck! Scoop!" shouted Bob, **"Quick! Grab onto the tower!"**

The tower **groaned** and tipped sideways. Brad slipped and only just managed to grab onto the railings! Muck and Scoop stopped the tower falling, while Lofty tried to reach Brad. But he wasn't tall enough!

"I was sure I'd put enough boulders in the foundations to make them secure," worried Bob.

"Oh, no!" thought Muck. **"It's my fault."** And he quickly told Bob what he'd done.

Muck asked Roley to help hold the tower. He rushed over to his castle and knocked it down. He grabbed the boulders and two solid planks of driftwood. He made them into a ramp for Lofty, so he could reach Brad and lift him to safety.

Muck worked hard to rebuild the foundations. Soon they were fixed. The tower was now safe and strong, and ready for Brad to climb once more ...

"Awesome!" shouted Brad, when he got to the top of the tower.

But suddenly he gasped, **"Something's in trouble!"**

"Oh, no!" shouted Muck. **"What!?"**

Your castle
- it needs
rebuilding!
Let's go!

SEASIDE Spotting

The machines had a great time at the beach.

Can you find these things in the big picture?
Tick [✓] each thing that you find.

surfboard ☐

sunshade ☐

seagull ☐

shells ☐

pineapple ☐

BRAD'S Beach Fun

**Brad Rad loves relaxing at the beach.
Can you guess what Brad is doing in this picture?
Join the dots to complete the picture, then colour it in.**

MATCH Muck

Find **2** pictures of Muck that are exactly the same.
Draw a line to join them up

1

4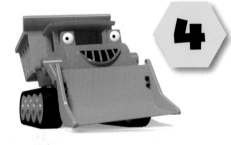

2

5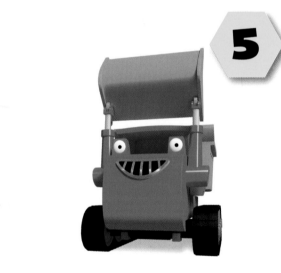

3

6

Did you know?
Muck loves to come first. But he loves being a part of Bob's team best of all.

THE Big Dig

Muck, Scoop and Scratch are the diggers on Bob's team. They call themselves the Diggers Three! Follow the tangled lines to discover what each digger finds when they dig a big hole for Bob.

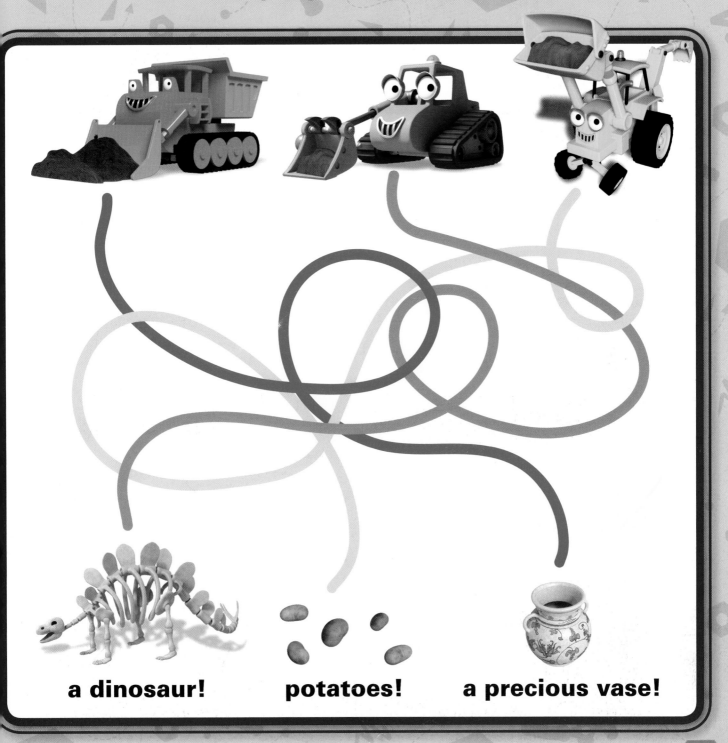

a dinosaur!   potatoes!   a precious vase!

SCRAMBLER
Gets Clean

You can help read this story. Join in when you see a picture.

Scrambler **Bob** **Muck** **forest**

 feels brave. He races through the and

scrambles over the hills to and the team. is

building the machines a new machine-wash!

"It will SQUIRT us with soapy water," says  ,

"SCRUB us with huge brushes and BLAST us with hot air."

"It's too scary," thinks  , "I will stay clean and shiny

so I never have to use the machine-wash."

 sends to pick up the new showerhead for the

machine-wash from the Supplier's Yard.

On the way back,  zooms through the but

there is a muddy puddle ahead.  screeches on his

brakes and stops just in time. But the showerhead falls into

the puddle!  doesn't want to get muddy but he

knows what he must do ...

... 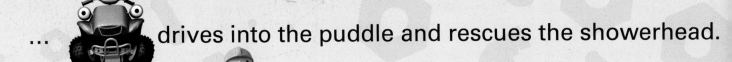 drives into the puddle and rescues the showerhead.

Back at the yard, fits the showerhead and says, "As you're

the dirtiest, , you can have the first wash."

"But, I'm scared," admits . "I thought I was brave but

I'm not."

"You are brave," replies , "brave to say that

you're scared."

 drives into the wash and soon rolls out shiny

and clean.

"Was it scary?" asks .

"No, it was fun!" says . "It was so much fun,

I'm going to have another go!"

FOREST Scramble

Start

Scrambler is rushing through the forest to do a job for Bob. Help Scrambler find a path through the trees to the other side of the forest.

Did you know?
Scrambler is the fastest machine in Bob's team.

Finish

TOOL Time

Circle the right tool to match the description.

The smallest hammer.

The biggest paint brush.

The longest saw.

The shortest trowel.

Answers on page 68.

GUESS Who?

Can you work out which of Bob's friends are being described?

1

I love wearing my blue hard hat and red earrings.

2

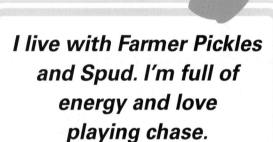

I live with Farmer Pickles and Spud. I'm full of energy and love playing chase.

3

If it's muddy or mucky, then I'm the machine for the job!

4

I'm always in a spin, whizzing around and around!

Answers on page 68. **39**

ROLEY'S Rovers

The machines were playing their favourite game – football!

"Goal!" everyone cheered, as the ball went in.

"What a team!" said Wendy. **"All you need now is a mascot."**

"What's a mascot?" asked Roley.

"It's someone who brings a football team good luck," Wendy explained.

Just then, Bob came hurrying into the yard. He had some exciting news for the team!

Mr Bentley had asked Bob and the machines to fix up the old Fixham Rovers football ground.

The machines gasped!

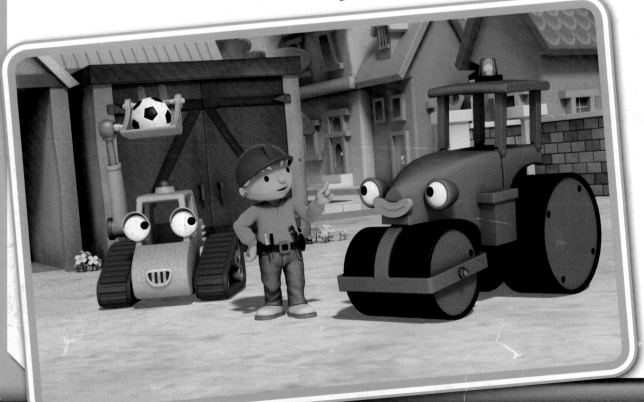

Mr Bentley came to the yard to discuss the job with Bob. There was going to be a match that afternoon, so the team would have to work fast!

"We'll fix it in time," promised Bob.

Before Mr Bentley left, he chanted with Bob:

**Fixham Rovers are the best –
Win or lose, they never rest!**

"What's that?" asked Roley.

"It's the team chant," explained Bob. **"The mascot sings it to cheer on the players."**

Bob gave everyone jobs to do. Scoop and Wendy were to fetch the goal posts, Scratch and Muck had to get the white paint, and Bob and Roley would make a start on the pitch.

When Bob and Roley got to the football field, they saw that it was a **real mess!** There was a big mound of earth at one end, molehills all over the turf, and the white lines marking the edges of the pitch were scuffed out and very faint.

Bob went through the plans with Roley, but Roley was too busy trying to think of new football chants to listen!

Just then Mr Bentley came by. He needed Bob's help to coach the team, ready for the match that afternoon.

When he saw Roley, he gasped! **"Roley is exactly the same colour as the Fixham Rovers team!"** he said, showing Bob and Roley his Fixham Rovers scarf.

"Perhaps I could be the Team Mascot?" asked Roley, nervously.

"It's a very important job," said Mr Bentley. **"You must sing very loudly, to cheer on the team."**

Roley promised to sing loudly, so it was agreed he would be the new Fixham Mascot!

Before he left, Bob asked Roley if he understood the plans for the pitch.

"Yeah, of course," muttered Roley, too excited to pay any attention.

Scoop, Muck and Scratch arrived to help Roley. They asked what the plan was, but Roley was too busy making up new chants to concentrate.

"Um, just move that mound of earth to the middle of the pitch," he said.

Scoop, Muck and Scratch got to work. As they rushed about, moving the earth, their wheels rubbed out the remaining white lines.

Soon they were finished, and stood back to admire their work. But it didn't look right. How would the footballers pass the ball over the big mound of earth in the middle of the pitch? And without the white lines, how would they know where to put the goals?

Just then, Bob arrived back. He was very surprised to see the pitch still in such a **mess!**

Roley was sorry. He asked Bob to see the plans again. Then he shouted as loudly as he could:

Come on, team,
Let's get it clean!
Let's make the pitch
Look a dream!

As the team worked, Roley kept on chanting. It helped the machines to work faster than ever! When all the earth had been cleared away, Bob and Wendy painted the white lines.

The pitch was finally finished – just in time for the match to be played.

"What a team," said Mr Bentley, **"and Roley, with chants like that, you're going to be a wonderful mascot for Fixham Rovers. With you cheering on the players, we'll be winners every time!"**

THE Roley Rap

Roley loves to sing as he works. Can you help him to finish a new rap, by filling in the missing words?

I roll away to get dirt flat,

And then I stop to have a .... **chip or chat?**

It's great to work alongside Bob,

As very soon we've done the .... **jam or job?**

Did you know?
Roley loves all animals. His best friend is Bird.

Answers on page 68.

FIND the Footballs

Bob and the team are having a kick-about.

How many footballs can you count in this picture?

Answers on page 68. **47**

SPOON Puppets

Tip

Make sure you match up the right head and arms for Bob and Wendy.

You will need:

- 2 wooden spoons
- Scissors
- Colouring crayons
- Glue or sticky tape

Idea

Why don't you put on a Bob and Wendy puppet show for your family?

QUICK Quiz

Can you help Spud decide if the statements are true or false? Circle the correct answers.
Good luck!

1 Roley is green.   True   False

2 Scruffty is a dog.   True   False

3 Dizzy is a dumper truck.   True   False

4 Bob wears a yellow hard hat.   True   False

5 Lofty is a cement mixer.   True   False

6 Wendy loves to lay bricks.   True   False

Answers on page 68.

SCRATCH
and the Bell

You can help read this story. Join in when you see a picture.

Scratch   **Bob**   **Ela**   **bell**   **Muck**

and the team are at the school. They're fixing the

roof for . needs a digger to go and do a job by

themselves, at Farmer Pickles' field.  asks to go. Only

a big digger is allowed to do jobs on their own, and

wants to be a big digger.

 gives  the old school to ring if he gets

lonely on his own. The other machines will come and get

 if they hear the . "But I won't get lonely,"

boasts , "I'm just like a big digger."

 starts digging, but it isn't long before he misses his

friends. doesn't ring the  because he thinks a

big digger wouldn't get lonely. Instead,  makes a new

friend out of mud. But the mud friend collapses on top of

 and he is stuck in the mud!  can't reach the

to call his friends for help!

The squirrels ring the for . Ring-a-ling,

ring-a-ling! and the other machines hear the bell

and rush to help . They pull out of the mud.

 tells them about being lonely and building a

mud friend.

"All diggers get lonely sometimes," says  , "but it

takes a big digger to admit it."

SCHOOL-time

Scratch, Bob and Wendy are visiting Ela and the children at the school. Can you spot **5** differences in picture 2?

1

2

Answers on page 68.

ODD One Out

Look very carefully at the pictures below.
Point to the odd one out in each row.

LOFTY'S Helpful Day

Bright and early, the machines were ready in the yard.

"Er, what are we doing today, Bob?" asked Lofty.

"Well, we're going to be very busy," said Bob. **"We've got to build an outside staircase for Mrs Toosey at the toy shop, as well as fixing Mr Bentley's roof."**

There was a lot to do and Bob was going to need help.

"I must be really helpful today," thought Lofty.

Lofty went to collect the railings for the staircase.

On his way to the Supplier's Yard, Lofty saw Farmer Pickles. Farmer Pickles was looking very **worried**. He had a fruit delivery to make, but he had lost Scruffty.

Lofty wanted to be really helpful. So he told Farmer Pickles he would deliver the fruit, while Farmer Pickles looked for Scruffty.

Lofty was very happy that he'd been so helpful. He just wasn't sure what to do first. He thought for a moment and then rushed off towards the Supplier's Yard.

Scruffty was with Spud. They were playing hide-and-seek.

"Ready or not," shouted Spud, **"here I come!"**

Scruffty barked and went to find somewhere to hide. He ran through the open door of Mrs Toosey's toy shop.

The door slammed behind him. Scruffty was trapped in the shop!

Meanwhile, Lofty was rushing to the Supplier's Yard. As he passed Mr Bentley's house he saw Wendy.

Wendy was up a tall ladder, fixing the roof.

"Oh, Lofty," said Wendy, **"can you help me with these roof tiles?"**

Lofty said he would. It felt nice being **so helpful**.

"I'll be right back," Lofty told Wendy. **"I'll just deliver this fruit."**

Lofty rushed away, but then suddenly remembered the railings! He turned around and dashed back to Mrs Toosey's toy shop.

At the toy shop Bob and Scoop were waiting for Lofty. They needed his help to build the top of the staircase.

As they waited they heard a **WOOF**. It was Scruffty! He had his nose pressed against the pane of an upstairs window. They tried the door, but it was shut and the key was inside.

Just then Lofty arrived back, puffing hard.

"Lofty!" said Bob. **"Thank goodness, we need your help. But what's all this fruit and where are the railings?"**

Lofty had been so busy trying to be helpful, that he'd forgotten to pick up the railings or to deliver Farmer Pickles' fruit!

Lofty explained how he'd wanted to be really helpful. **"But now I could do with some help myself,"** he said, sadly.

"That's no problem!" said Bob, kindly. **"I think you just tried to do too many things at once."**

Bob sent Scratch to deliver the fruit, Muck to get the railings and Scoop to help Wendy.

Lofty felt sad. He wasn't helping anyone now.

"But I need your help with the most important job," said Bob. **"We must rescue Scruffty!"**

Lofty lifted Bob up, so he could reach the window. Bob carefully undid the frame and lifted away the glass. Then he picked up Scruffty, and Lofty lowered them to safety.

Lofty and Bob put the window back and then quickly finished building the staircase.

Farmer Pickles arrived and saw Scruffty.

"You found him!" he said happily, giving Scruffty a big hug.

Bob explained how they had rescued Scruffty. **"And I couldn't have done it without Lofty's help,"** he said.

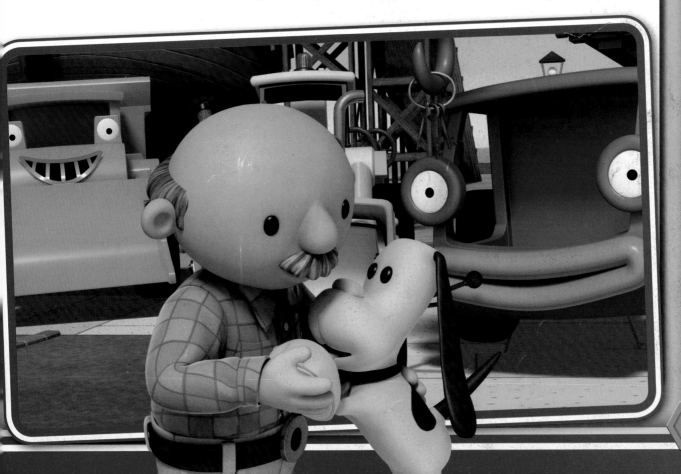

LOFTY'S Jobs

Lofty is in a muddle again! He must deliver the objects below, but he can't remember who they are for.

Help Lofty decide where to take each thing. Draw a line from the cake, paint pot and flowers to either David Mockney, Scoop or Wendy.

cake

paint pot

flowers

David Mockney

Scoop

Wendy

A Present for Spud

Lucky Spud! Mrs Toosey is letting him choose a toy from her shop as a birthday present.

What sort of toy do you think Spud would like? Draw your ideas in the box.

RACE Around Fixham

Start

You forgot Mr Mockney's paint. Go back to **START**.

Get to Toosey's Toy Shop before it closes. Rush on **2 spaces**.

Take a shortcut through Farmer Pickles' field.

A football match is starting. Hurry on **2 spaces**.

Relax on the beach. Move back **2 spaces**.

The machines are rushing home to Bob's yard. See who can get there first!

You will need a dice and a counter for each person playing. The first person to roll a 6 starts. Take turns to roll the dice and move your counters. The first counter to reach the Finish wins!

Finish

Take a detour to the Supplier's Yard. Go back 1 space.

The lights are green. Move on 1 space.

The lights are red. Move back 1 space.

Take Ela to school. Move on 2 spaces.

67

ANSWERS

Page 20 Colour Mix-up!

Page 28 Seaside Spotting

Page 29 Brad's Beach Fun
Brad is surfing!

Page 30 Match Muck
*Pictures **3** and **4** of Muck are exactly the same.*

Page 31 The Big Dig
Muck finds a precious vase, Scratch finds a dinosaur and Scoop finds potatoes.

Page 36 Forest Scramble

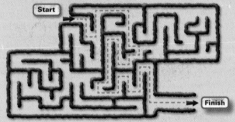

Page 38 Tool Time!

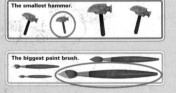

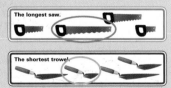

Page 39 Guess Who?

1 *is Wendy,* **2** *is Scruffty,* **3** *is Muck,* **4** *is Dizzy.*

Page 46 The Roley Rap
The right words are **chat** *and* **job**.

Page 47 Find the Footballs
There are **5** *footballs hidden in the picture.*

Page 51 Quick Quiz
1-True, *2-True,* *3-False,* *4-True,* *5-False,* *6-True.*

Page 56 School-time

Page 57 Odd One Out

Page 64 Lofty's Jobs
The cake is for Wendy, the paint pot is for David Mockney and the flowers are for Scoop.

JOIN BOB'S BUSY TEAM

WITH

Bob the Builder ™

NEW LOOK MAGAZINE

LOOK! HOLIDAY BUMPER GIFT!

ROCK and roll!

Bob the Builder

COLOURING! PUZZLES! STORIES!

GIANT pull-out PLAY POSTER!

FUN machines WORKBOOK!

HAVE FUN WITH US!

OVER 50 COOL STICKERS

on sale every **4** weeks

REAL machines

FANTASTIC GIFTS AND STICKERS!

PLUS

PUZZLES   FUN WORKBOOK   STORIES